BLOCKCHAIN AND BITCOIN FUNDAMENTALS

The Ultimate Step By Step Guide To Understanding Blockchain and Bitcoin

Disclaimer

The sole purpose of this book is to provide information. The information contained in this book is provided on an as is basis, and the author is not responsible for the accuracy of information provided in the book.

The content within this book has been derived from various sources. The reader should consult professionals before implementing any advice mentioned in the book. Under no circumstances will any blame or legal responsibility be held against the publisher, or author, for any damages, reparation, or monetary loss due to the information contained within this book.

Investing and trading in cryptocurrencies involves considerable risk of loss and is not suitable for every investor. The value of a cryptocurrency may fluctuate, causing investors to lose more than their original investment. You should not engage in cryptocurrency trading if you don't fully understand how the transactions work and your level of risk with each transaction.

Table of Contents

CHAPTER 1
INTRODUCTION

Brief History of the Blockchain

Blockchain is one of the biggest innovations of the century, with some experts going as far as comparing it with the creation of the internet itself. With the blockchain, there is substance behind the hype: in a matter of 10 years, the technology has gone from zero to being the underlying technology for serious alternatives to traditional banking and personal finance options.

Origins of The Blockchain

While Bitcoin is the first and the most prominent chapter in the mainstream history of the blockchain, the actual history of blockchain goes a bit beyond the innovation of Bitcoin. The concept we call blockchain today is a result of the work of cryptographer colleagues: Stuart Haber and W. Scott Stornetta. Their work, titled How to Time-Stamp a Digital Document" was published in 1991. They set out to create a chain of blocks with cryptographic security to eliminate the possibility of tampering with the document timestamps. By 1992, they had incorporated the Merkle trees structure, which allows for collection of a larger quantity of documents per blockchain block, because the structure enables efficient and secure verification of content in a large body of data.

In an interview with Breaker mag.com, Stornetta said that their initial goal of creating an immutable ledger lead to "a naive solution," as it had a "digital safety-deposit box" for recording the time and date when a document was created, but the scheme did not have anything to prevent the time-stamping service to collude with clients.

Changing their goal after the initial failure, they decided to disprove the concept of immutable ledger, but, this time, they ended up with a distributed immutable ledger. In 1994, the duo founded Surety, a company that offered time-stamping services utilizing the first-ever blockchain. However, they did not have a purely digital ledger. Instead, they posted client hashes in New York Times's "Notices & Lost and Found" section.

Satoshi Nakamoto

One of the main figures in the history of the blockchain is, of course, the founder of Bitcoin, Satoshi Nakamoto. A person whose true identity is still a mystery, Santoshi Nakamoto wrote the code for Bitcoin in 2007 and published a white paper in

2008 on bitcoin.org. In the white paper, he proposes his solution for the double spending problem of financial transactions and how it can end the need for third parties for digital transactions. According to the white paper, "the peer to peer version of electronic cash would allow online payments to be sent directly from one party to another going through a financial institution, message access a trusted third party to prevent double spending." The paper details how the technology would work, and mentions the benefits of the solution, including simplified payment verification and enhanced privacy. Nakamoto formed the genesis block, and other blocks are mined from the genesis block. Bitcoin was released to the general public in 2009.

A lesser known figure related to Bitcoin, Gavin Anderson is a web developer who played a central role in the development of Bitcoin. Essentially, he took over the project after Nakamoto. In his final communication with the public on the subject of Bitcoin, Nakamoto commented about Gavin Aderson and said that Bitcoin is in "good hands."

Separation of the Blockchain and Bitcoin

Another important step in the history of the blockchain was its separation from Bitcoin. The Ethereum development stage involves the development of a blockchain that overcomes the limitation of Bitcoin and is capable of performing various functions. The person leading this development was a Russian-Canadian programmer Vitalik

Buterin. This initiative resulted in the birth of the Ethereum blockchain in 2013 and its official launch two years later in 2015.

The Ethereum blockchain is known for its ability to support development of a wide range of applications and a special type of contract called the smart contract (explained later in the chapter). The blockchain is a leader in terms of daily transactions, and it's also widely used as the underlying technology for many digital tokens.

New Applications

Blockchain Technology continues to evolve and several new applications of the technology have come to the fore in the last few years. Some of these new applications include Hyperledger, NEO and EOS.IO. One of the most recent applications of the blockchain technology is Facebook's cryptocurrency project called Libra. The project is supported by major players including Visa, Uber and Spotify, but has run into a lot of controversy because of Facebook's record with data privacy.

CHAPTER 2 THE BLOCKCHAIN ARCHITECTURE

Layers of The Blockchain

In terms of the architecture of a blockchains, we can divide it into the following layers:

1. **Application:** The transactions are processed in this layer.
2. **Networking:** Transactions and consensus messages are spread in this layer.
3. **Consensus:** Allows nodes to agree on the present state of the system.

Centralized vs. Decentralized Architecture

One of the key differentiators between blockchain types is whether they are centralized or decentralized. Let's take a look at how decentralization and centralization differ from each other and the benefits of both.

Decentralization

Decentralization means that there is no central body or authority to control the cryptocurrency. "Decentralized" is what many people consider to be an essential attribute of a blockchain network. However, decentralization is not a given with blockchains, as we will discuss later on.

In a decentralized cryptocurrency network, the data and the whole infrastructure depends on nodes (transaction validators) that directly communicate with each other. In other words, users can be confident that there is no one with the authority to influence the network and affect the transactions taking place on it.

The transactions between parties are recorded on a ledger which the masternodes maintain. Here it is important to understand the difference between a node and master node.

Node vs. Masternode

A node is any computer participating in ensuring the integrity of the cryptocurrency network. For a currency like Bitcoin, for instance, there are several people running nodes from across the globe. However, not all nodes can maintain a copy of the coins in the ledger. This is where a master node comes in to the picture. A masternode is a computer (digital wallet) that has an entire copy of the ledger in real time. For providing this service, the master node is rewarded with crypto coins.

The amount of money you can earn as a masternode depends on multiple factors, including the coin you choose, the protocol defining the masternode's compensation, the performance of the coin in the market. People looking to run masternodes have several options, including, but not limited to Dash, Chaincoin, Zcoin, and SmartCash.

According to Chaincoin, to become a masternode, you have to invest 1000 Chaincoin. The reward you receive is currently 20% of each mined block reward and transaction fees. The general steps for setting up a masternode are as follows:

- Buy coins from an exchange to join the project.
- Install a desktop wallet and synchronize with the blockchain.
- Transfer the coins to the wallet.
- Create an address in the wallet and send the coins to that address.
- Setup the node at your location or virtually.
- Run the server and synchronize with blockchain.
- Set up your master node on your desktop wallet.
- Earn rewards

Benefits of Decentralization

One of the main benefits of decentralization is that it reduces the likelihood of fraud. The information is distributed to computers all over the globe, so it becomes difficult to manipulate the information. Another advantage is that the currencies can survive unusual events taking place in the country or region because they don't depend on the resources available in that region – think power outages or political issues. The fact that many crypto coins are not backed by metals, such as gold and silver, or fiat currencies means that a fall in these assets' price does not affect investors. Developers of cryptocurrencies have also made them so that they are easy to use and manage: investors can easily store their coins on their mobile phones and not have to worry about the procedures and fees associated with traditional banking.

Centralization

The other main type of cryptocurrency projects are those who prefer to have a centralized authority. With these exchanges, you will still be trusting a third party, like you do with traditional banking. An attribute you will find common in many centralized cryptocurrencies is that the body in control owns a large portion of their crypto assets. Some notable centralized crypto projects include IOTA, Ripple, and NEO.

Benefits of Centralization

So what could be the benefit of moving away from traditional banking into another centralized system? You will be surprised to know that the majority of new investors invest in centralized projects. While decentralization may offer more security and control, established big early blockchain adopters tend to lean towards blockchains that have central management. Combine this with the fact that governments are still trying to figure out how to regulate the cryptocurrency market, and you get a clearer picture of the current market. In terms of the trading options available with centralized and decentralized exchanges, centralized ones usually offer cryptocurrency-cryptocurrency pairs.

Public vs. Private Blockchains

Another important concept to grasp about blockchain is the difference between public and private blockchains. The main difference between the two is that users need to take permission to join a private blockchain network and public blockchain networks don't require any permissions. In other words, the level of access you get is different.

On a public network, you can start verification or mining activities without any restrictions to your access to that network. On a private blockchain, to become a miner or node, you will go through a selection process and there will be specific rights and restrictions. Popular network Ethereum and Bitcoin are public, while Ripple and Hyperledger are private. Another term used for private blockchains is "permissioned" blockchains because of the processes they follow. Let's take a look at the benefits and disadvantages of public and private blockchains.

Benefits and Drawbacks of Public Blockchains

Public blockchains are decentralized, have a large number of validating nodes, which make them a secure system. Transparency is another advantage. Transaction data is available to the public and anyone can verify the validity of transactions. The system is also a trustless, as it removes the need to place trust in intermediaries.

Some disadvantages of public blockchains include slowness, highway energy consumption, and scalability. Public blockchains like Bitcoin and Ethereum are slow, because with their consensus mechanisms, it takes for the network to reach consensus, and you can only fit a certain number of transactions in a block of the blockchain. To give you an idea of the difference in speed, the Ethereum blockchain has a transaction speed of 15 transactions per second, while the transaction speeds of a centralised payment processor such as Visa is about 1700 transactions per second.

Another issue is the use of electricity. Bitcoin's proof of work (PoW) mechanism consumes more than 7 gigawatts of electricity according to the Cambridge Bitcoin Electricity Consumption Index (CBECI). This equates to 64 terawatt hours of energy per year, which is higher than the annual energy use of Switzerland (58.4 TwH) and close to Austria (64.6 TwH). This number puts Bitcoin's energy consumption at 0.25% of the world's electricity consumption.

However, there are some other mechanisms in use that aren't as electricity-heavy. For example, the proof of stake (PoS) mechanism consumes less energy than PoW (explanation in Chapter 2). The energy cost of a typical Ethereum transaction is lower than Bitcoin, but they also use PoW so the energy consumption is still very significant. However, the Ethereum Foundation has plans to reduce energy consumption by switching to PoS by the end of this year. It's important to remember that the transactions themselves do not use a lot of computational power, so the move towards an effective but leaner consensus system can help can with computational power use. Large consumption of electricity is also problematic for minors, because electricity companies may place higher tariffs on miners compared to the general public.

Third concern with public networks is that of scalability. Traditional systems have the capacity to handle large amounts of participants, but public blockchains tend to get bogged down with an increase in participants. However, this problem may be rectified in the future as many developers are focused on solving this issue.

Benefits and Drawbacks of Private Blockchains

As mentioned before, private blockchains have restrictions on the functions participants can perform. This is beneficial in a few ways. Firstly, a private blockchain has participants who can be verified, similar to a private business. To join the network the participant must provide an authentic proposal and the blockchain must confirm the person. This confirmation is done by a set protocol or by network operators. Also, because of the fewer participants, it takes less time to achieve consensus. This means that more transactions can be processed. The processing speed of private blockchain can be in the thousands.

Another advantage of private networks is scalability. These networks have fewer nodes that authorise the data, so the network can support more transactions. The decision making process is also centralised; therefore, it's faster. Ripple is a prominent example of a private blockchain. The network has XRP as its native cryptocurrency, and it has the capacity to process about 1500 transactions per second. Also, Ripple has the capacity to scale to the level of payment processing that large processors can offer (50,000 TPS for Visa).

The presence of a third party means that you have to trust in the ability of the nodes present in the system. Trusting nodes is a disadvantage because the number of nodes are lesser, so the risk of someone manipulating the network is higher compared to public networks. Also, unlike the public blockchain you cannot check the validity by yourself.

CHAPTER 3 HOW THE BLOCKCHAIN WORKS?

Cryptography

Cryptography, also called cryptology, is the process of manipulating data in a way that it becomes impossible for an unauthorised user to read it. In order to read transmitted information, the user will need a decryption key. Besides enabling information to maintain integrity in transmission from sender to the receiver and storage, cryptography also enables you to verify who sent the message and if the message was delivered or not.

Encryption Algorithms

The parties involved in a transaction authenticate each other by using key pairs. There are many encryption algorithms used for cryptography today, including Public Key Cryptography (PKC), Secret Key Cryptography (SKC) and hash functions.

Public Key Cryptography (PKC)

Anthony Owens

In PKC, two keys are used. One key is accessible to everyone, while the other key is accessible to the owner. To encrypt the information, the sender will use the public key of the receiver. And to decrypt the information, the receiver uses their private key. Here it is important to mention the concept of non-repudiation. In case of digital security, nonrepudiation is a way that the information sender cannot later deny that they sent the information. With PKC, the sender uses a private key to encrypt plain text, and the receiver utilizes the sender's public key for decrypting the message.

Secret Key Cryptography (SKC)

Also called symmetric encryption, only one key is used for encrypting and decrypting the message.

Hash Functions

Hash functions don't use a key. They are basically an algorithm for individual files or passwords to verify their authenticity. The value produced by running an algorithm is called a checksum. Widely used hash functions, including SHA-1 and MD5. Modern programming languages contains several hash functions. (More on hash functions in the next topic in the next section in the chapter).

Threat to Encryption

While encryption algorithms make it hard for attackers to decrypt information, this does not mean that there aren't any threats to the immutability of the blockchain.

51% Attack

One of the widely known threats is the 51% attack. In a blockchain network, participants who have computing power can in theory gain a controlling interest in even a distributed, decentralized block-chain. In practical terms, miners can by themselves or collectively control over 50% of the network's mining hash rate for computing power. This would allow attackers to stop new transactions from getting validation, reverse transactions, enabling double spending of coins.

To explain the 51% attack, let's consider the ex-ample of Bitcoin. A new block is generated roughly every 10 minutes. After the block is finalized, no one can alter it because the altered version of the public ledger would be rejected by the network users. Attackers having majority of the computing power can prevent miners from completing blocks, which in theory allow attacker to have a monop-oly over the mining process and gain all the rewards associated with the mining process. They can also double spend Bitcoins, which means that they can send a coin and make it appear that they never sent it, so they still have it.

Blockchain Consensus Protocols

Protocols are used to define the size of a blocks, the rewards for miners, etc. The two most well-known protocols are proof of work (PoW) and proof of stake (PoS).

A new transaction is performed on the blockchain the data is stored in a new block. This new block and become a part of the blockchain, the information is verified by creating a hash. This is a 256-bit number for identifying the data in the block. The hash is also known as the digital fingerprint of the data. Computers within the blockchain network are able to create hash values by solving a math puzzle. This process of finding a solution to the puzzle and assigning a hash value is called mining.

To explain this concept, let's consider two blocks: block 1 and block 2. Miners collect transaction data for block 1 and give it a value hash 1. For the next block in the chain, they repeat the process and give it a new value hash 2. Hash 2 will have hash 1 and new hash based on the new transactions. Since one block contains the information of the other block, if data is changed in one block, it will change the hash of that block and also all the blocks that follow it. In other words, you will have to modify the entire blockchain to make changes to the stored information. Therefore, it's very difficult to hack a blockchain.

PoW vs. PoS Consensus

The example given above is a proof-of-work system. The hash block created as a result of the mining process is the proof-of-work for the miners of the cryptocurrency. The idea of someone overpowering the network with a 51% attack was mentioned by Satoshi Nakamoto in the Bitcoin white paper. As a solution to prevent this problem, he proposed a PoW system. While Bitcoin has given prominence to this concept, it existed before cryptocurrencies. The term first appeared in a 1999 paper by Marcus Jacobson and Arya Jewels.

Proof of Stake systems are also used to validate transactions by creating a new hash; however, the difference in the two systems is the process of getting the rewards. In a PoS system, there is no competition among the nodes for the reward. So how does a node validate transactions? The node goes through a selection process in which the selection criterion is how much stake the node has in the network. The lack of competition for validating nodes has certain benefits. Firstly, the energy consumption is lower since less computing power is being used per transaction data validation for solving the math puzzle.

Another feature of the PoS system is that there are no miners in this network because there are no coins to be mined. All the coins that will be part of the network are created before hand. Therefore, people who work are called "forgers" instead of miners. Forgers are paid a transaction fee. This fee is for sending transactions across the network.

To make the process fairer for the nodes, some additional processes are added to the system. One of these is the randomised block selection process. In this process, selection is based on a combination of the highest stake and the lowest hash value. Another method is the coin age selection process. This method gives value to how long user has put their tokens at stake. The coin age calculation includes the days the coins have been at stake into total number of coins. Of course, the exact methods used vary from cryptocurrency to cryptocurrency.

Having skin in the game in the form of coins at stake is a motivation factor to not validate fraudulent transactions. Involvement in fraud, results in the forger losing their stake along with the ability to work as a forger for the blockchain network.

Other consensus protocols include proof of authority (PoA), proof of capacity, etc. In a PoA system, a single private key has the authority to create blocks. Selection is based on the value of identities. In other words, validators are putting their reputation on the line instead of coins. In a PoA consensus system, the validators need to confirm their real identity. At the same time, they must invest money. The method for selecting validators needs to be equal for all candidates.

Soft Fork vs Hard Fork
A "fork," in programming language means an open-

source modification of the code. All software needs to be updated to improve performance or fix problems. These updates change the working of the cryptocurrency's protocol. The code after the fork is like the unmodified code, but with important changes. When we talk about the use of forks in crypto projects, they are normally used for making fundamental changes, or for creating an asset that is like the original. The versions of the blockchain before and after the fork have a shared history, meaning that the record of transactions remains the same on the new and old versions.

Forks can be intentional and unintentional. An unintentional fork happens when nodes do not replicate the same information. Unintentional folks are generally identified. The reason for most of the intentional forks is a disagreement between users about embedded characteristics.

Soft Fork

A soft fork is a backward-compatible change in the protocol. Nodes belonging to the old version can process blocks created in the new version as long as they abide by the new protocol. However, the new version will not be able to process blocks from the older version when the fork is performed to tighten the rules of the protocol.

Let's consider the example of a soft fork which shrinks the size of individual blocks making up the blockchain. The older version of the blockchain will still be able to accommodate the smaller size blocks, but the new version will not accept the larger blocks of the older version, because the new protocol has shrunk the acceptable size for the blocks.

After the fork, if the new version of the blockchain network takes off, it would make the older version less attractive to investors because the new version blocks are compatible with both the pre-fork and post-fork versions, unlike the old version. There are several examples of soft forks of cryptocurrencies. In case of bitcoin, the 1 MB limit on block size was done as soft work.

Soft forks are non-reversible. The only way you can reverse this fork is by a hard fork. An advantage a soft fork has over a hard fork is that there is less possibility of double spending. This is because users with the pre-fork version can identify both new and old blocks, which is not the case with hard fork.

Hard Fork

A hard fork is a non-backward compatible change in the cryptocurrency protocol. It does not allow older nodes to continue processing and pushing new blocks. If an older version is in use after the fork, they will have a separate protocol than the newer version, which can cause confusion.

Hard forks are performed for various reasons. In some cases, they are required for making improvements to the existing protocol. In other cases, they are used to create an independent protocol and blockchain.

Consider the example where the protocol is changed to increase the size of the block. An old node will not be able to process a transaction because it does not agree with the protocol, so the node will reject the new block. Let's say that the next block in this chain is validated by older not because it meets the size requirements of the old protocol. This would lead to two versions of the blockchain – one has only the older blocks and the other has new and old blocks.

The problem of double spending arises with hard forks because the cryptocurrency spent in the new version can also be spent in the older version, because the old nodes will not be able to detect transactions taking place in the new version. A possible solution to this problem is that one branch is given preference over the other. Another option is that nodes in the older version switch to the newer version. In case of Bitcoin, the solution was a splitting of bitcoin into Litecoin and Bitcoin Cash, as discussed later in the book.

It's important to note that hard forks can be planned or forced. With a planner fork, users upgrade to the new version, abandoning the older one. Forced situations usually happen when there is a disagreement within the participants about whether there should be an upgrade. Normally, in these cases, there is a splitting of the protocol into two different blockchains which are incompatible with each other. The supporters of both projects continue to develop their preferred version of the cryptocurrency.

The transactions from the original blockchain are not lost in case of a hard fork. The amount of coins you have before the fork will be what you get with the new cryptocurrency.

Smart Contracts

"Smart contracts are self-executing contracts with the terms of the agreement between buyer and seller being directly written into lines of code. The code and the agreements contained therein exist across a distributed, decentralized blockchain network" (Investopedia). In practical terms, smart contracts allow users to exchange anything of value (money, property, etc.) in a transparent way without a middleman facilitating the transaction.

The term was first described by cryptographer Nick Szabo in 1994 as a tool for securing computer networks by using protocols with user interfaces. He considered these contracts to have potential applications in different sectors, including payment processing and credit systems. In terms of blockchain tech, smart contracts are an application program that works as a digital agreement created under certain rules. All nodes on the network follow rules set for smart contracts so there is consistency with digital agreements taking place on that network. This ensures that if the conditions defined in the protocol are not present, the contract will not be approved. Smart contracts give users the peace of mind they don't have to trust someone with their transaction.

Smart contracts have become synonymous with Ethereum, but they existed with Bitcoin as well. To explain how smart contracts work, let's consider the example of smart contracts on the Ethereum Virtual Machine (EVM). (It's important to mention the specific blockchain network when talking about smart contracts, because different networks may run their own smart contracts.)

How Smart Contracts Work

The first thing you should know about smart contracts is that they are not well represented by their name, because they are not any form of legal contract, nor are they smart in the technical sense of the word. In essence, these contracts are code that runs on a distributed system. Talking about smart contracts, Ethereum founder Vitalik Buterin says that they involve "determination of whether the asset should go to one person or back to the other person, or whether it should be immediately refunded to the person who sent it or some combination thereof."

Ethereum network uses smart contracts for executing and managing operations. The smart contract has a contract code and two keys. The user who creates the contract provides the first key. The other key is a digital identifier of the contract between the two parties. This identifier is unique to the smart contract. Any address on the network that is not a smart contract is an externally owned account (EOA). Users control EOAs.

It's not possible to add new functions to smart contracts on the Ethereum network; however, it is possible to delete a smart contract. For this to happen, the user who created the smart contract must include the "SELFDESTRUCT" function in the code. The tokens on the Ethereum blockchain followed the ERC 20 standard and are called ERC 20 tokens. Many blockchain companies issue their tokens on the Ethereum network. let's look at why companies like smart contracts.

However, there is the option of choosing an upgradeable smart contract. To understand this attribute, let's considered the example where one smart contract is divided into many contracts. For some of these contracts, you include the self-destruct function in the code and for others you don't. This would leave you with a smart contract that has some deletable parts and other functions that are immutable.

Benefits of Smart Contracts

The first benefit is trust. The documents are on a shared ledger and there is no possibility of losing the document. Autonomy is another major advantage. You don't have to go to any broker or lawyer to ensure that the transaction is valid. Smart contracts are also very versatile, which makes their application easier in different services and for different solutions. Besides organizing assets, smart contracts are also being used for creating crypto wallets and decentralized exchanges. As mentioned before, the speed of processing transactions varies a lot depending on the protocol and system. Smart contracts are much faster when compared to manual processing of documents. Besides being faster, the use of software code and automation also means that there is less possibility of errors.

Smart contracts provide many benefits. However, the code is written by humans so there is always the possibility of errors, especially if the code is not written by an experienced programmer. Another disadvantage is related to the immutable nature of these contracts. One example of the challenges with immutability is the 2016 hacking of Decentralized Autonomous Organization (DAO). This resulted in the loss of millions of ether ETH (worth $50 million). The code developers were not able to fix the flaws in the smart code that enables the hacking because the contracts were immutable. The incident caused the community to perform a hard fork that gives us Ethereum, the new version, and Ethereum Classic, the old version.

Another problem is with the legal definition of smart contracts. While in the future we may see legal forms using smart contracts instead of traditional contracts, now, there isn't much information about the legal status of smart contracts in a legal framework.

Smart contracts are deterministic, terminable and isolated. In the deterministic type of contract, the output is always the same for a given input. For example, 9 + 1 will always be 10 on all computers. Terminable means that the contract will terminate within a given time limit. To ensure termination, developers can, for example, put a fee on each instruction and terminate when the prepaid fee for performing instructions is paid. Setting a predetermined time limit is another method. You can also ensure termination by making sure that the blockchain cannot start an endless loop. the isolation feature is important because anyone can upload a smart contract, and a bad contract may affect the whole network.

Cryptocurrency Wallet

A cryptocurrency wallet stores your public and private keys and interacts with blockchain networks.

In broad terms, there are two types of wallets – a hot wallet and a cold wallet. Hot wallets are connected to the internet. You can access the hard wallet anytime. Examples of hot wallets include software wallets, cloud wallets, most mobile wallets, and cryptocurrency exchanges. A cold wallet is not connected to the internet. You can receive funds in your cold wallet at any time but it's not possible to transfer these funds. Based on their functionality, cold wallets are mostly used for holding onto cryptocurrencies, while hot wallets are used for trading crypto assets. Cold wallets are a better option for storing coins because they are less susceptible to hack attacks, as they are offline and use a physical medium for storing the keys.

Before explaining the choices you have with wallets, let's look at how crypto wallets work. Many people misunderstand how crypto wallets work. Digital wallets are different from pocket wallets because they don't store currency. The concept of currency storage is different also because currencies are not stored in any single place. What is stored on the blockchain is the record of transactions that took place.

When someone sends you a digital currency, they are basically sending the asset to your wallet's address or public key. This address is an alphanumeric identifier. In technical terms, this address is a certain "location" on the blockchain where you can send the money. You can only use the money sent to you if the private key you have in your wallet matches the public address to which the sender sent the money. It's important to remember here that you shouldn't share your private key because it's used to sign transactions and prove ownership of the public key. If there's a match, you and the sender will see a change in your balance accordingly. The funds are always on the blockchain. In case you cannot use your wallet, you can still access your cryptocurrencies from another wallet if you have the private key.

Software Wallets

There are several types of software wallets, with the majority being hot wallets. Here are the three most important types of software wallets:

Web Wallets

Web wallets enable users to connect to the blockchain via a browser, so you don't have to install or download anything. Web wallets include wallets associated with exchanges and other browser wallet companies. Most web wallets allow you to set your password (private key) to access the wallets. However, some wallet companies hold and manage your private keys themselves.

Access to information about the private key is important with wallets. Letting the wallet provider manage your key may be more convenient for you if you're new, but it can be problematic. If you don't keep your private key to yourself, you're placing your trust in a third-party. One way of rectifying this issue is by offering shared control of the keys. Before selecting a wallet, check the company's rules about private keys.

Some well-known web wallets include MyEther-Wallet, LiteVault, GateHub, and MetaMask. Some wallets will support a specific currency, like Meta-Mask supports only ETH, while others will have a wider range, as is the case with GateHub, which supports BTC, BCH, XRP, ETH, DASH, XAU, etc.

To explain what to look for with wallets, let's consider the example of MyEtherWallet. This wallet is a combination of a web wallet and a desktop wallet because you create it online but store your information and assets on your computer. This gives you the advantage of accessibility through a web browser and the security of not storing your coins online. The wallet is compatible with several other wallets. In terms of costs, there are no fees for using the wallet, but you are charged a transaction fee for sending Ether. MyEtherWallet is compatible with ETH, ETC and ERC-20 tokens only.

Mobile Wallets

Designed specifically for smartphones, mobile wallets are a convenient way of performing cryptocurrency transactions. They have QR code functionality and are a good option for daily transactions. A precaution you should take with mobile apps is to have good malware protection. It's also a good idea to have a backup for the private keys and encrypt the wallet by using a strong password.

Generally, some of the top "mobile wallets" currently in use are specific to the operating system on which you can use them. These include Samsung Pay, Apple Pay, etc. In the world of cryptocurrencies, however, being operating-system specific is not the case. Some top wallets like Jaxx, Coinomi, Coinbase, and Blockchain are available for both iOS and Android systems.

A wallet like Jaxx is known for offering a large set of features and an adjustable speed for the transaction. It supports many coins and tokens. However, the app does not have the security features that some of its competitors provide. When buying a wallet for your cryptocurrencies, make sure you do a comparison of products.

Desktop Wallets

Another option we have is to download the wallet onto your computer, and from there use it in the same way you use it on your mobile. With desktop wallets you will be responsible for holding and managing your keys and assets. To encrypt the wallet, you will need to enter your password every time you run the software. And, if you lose the password you will lose access to your assets. Of course, you also have to consider the possibility of something happening to your computer in the case of desktop wallets. To protect yourself in case of a computer malfunction or theft, you can export the private key so you can access your assets on other devices.

There are several options available with desktop wallets as well. One of the popular ones is Electrum. The wallet is compatible with Mac OS, Linux, and Windows. Other notable desktop wallets include

Bitcoin Core, Exodus, Copay, and Atomic Wallet.

Hardware Wallets

Generally considered to be more secure than web wallets, a hardware wallet is a physical, electronic device that stores your keys and is not connected to the internet (cold wallet). The wallet uses a random number generator (RNG) system for creating your public and private keys. In practical terms, a hardware wallet allows you to plug the USB, or other device containing the key, into your computer, log in, do the transaction, and unplug. The offline storage keeps the key protected from hackers; however, you should make sure that the firmware is installed properly.

Some of the main things to consider with hard wallets are the price point, accessibility, and safety. Compared to online options, you will be looking at a higher price with the hardware wallet. Accessibility will also be different than a hot wallet. However, some platforms allow you to directly connect your device through them and do your trades. As with any portable device, you will need to protect it from getting lost or stolen. For security, the wallets are usually PIN-protected, and you can recover what you have in case the wallet is lost.

A hardware wallet is ideal for people who want to hold onto funds for a length of time. Some of the main players in this niche include Ledger Nano S, Ledger Blue, and TREZOR. To understand hardware wallet features, let's take the example of Ledger Nano S. The device supports over 1000 cryptocurrencies. It has an organic LED (OLED) screen that helps you double-check transactions.

The Ledger Nano S does not directly connect to the computer like a USB, but it comes with a USB cable. Besides the device and cable, a standard package has a lanyard, keychain, keyring and a recovery sheet for writing down the seed (words for recovering your account in case you lose the wallet). To set up the wallet for transactions, you will connect it to your computer using the USB cable, then select a PIN and backup your recovery phrase. Finally, you will install the Ledger app or integrate with a software wallet.

Paper Wallets
Paper wallets take the concept of hardware wallets to the next level. It is simply a piece of paper on which you print your crypto address and private key as QR codes. To send the money from the wallet, you will have to use a software wallet, manually giving your private key. To receive money through the wallet, you send money to the public key printed on the paper. With some paper wallets, you can download code and create new public and private keys for yourself offline.

While paper wallets are secure, they do have their flaws. One of the most glaring flaws is that they are not suitable for partial transactions. For instance, if you import your private key into a desktop wallet to spend a portion of your funds, the remaining funds will go to a "change address." Most software wallets set the change address to one you control, unlike paper wallets, where you will be responsible for doing this. Another thing here is that your paper wallet will be good for a transaction only, so you will need another one for future use. Like hardware wallets, there is, of course, the concern of the wallet getting damaged or lost. Bitaddress.org and WalletGenerator.net are two well-known paper wallet websites.

How to Pick a Wallet

To summarize, here are the features you should consider when searching for a wallet:

Wallet Type: Each type mentioned above has its own pros and cons. you will have to decide the factors you considered to be most important. Are you looking to hold the currency for the long term or looking to perform transactions conveniently on a regular basis?

Security: On the topic of security, we should look for differentiating factors such as 2-factor authentication, wallet security history, and offline versus online storage options provided by the company.

Easy Usability: Ease of use is also an important feature. If you are new to digital currency management or just want a smooth experience, then one that is easy to set up and use may be more important than one with an in-wallet exchange, for instance.

Currency: Currency related options are of course a must. Check which cryptocurrencies the wallet supports. Is there an option to store multiple currencies or does the company focus on a currency? Does the wallet have an option to exchange between currencies you are holding in it?

Public Opinion: Crypto wallets have been in use for long enough to have a public-led comparison between the different services on offer. Check what the community says about the wallet.

Cost: Last but not the least is the cost factor. While cost is not a big factor when it comes to most wallets price tag, it's important in the form of transaction fees or cost to buy the equipment.

Tokenization

Tokenization is an important concept to grasp if you are learning about crypto currencies. It is basically the conversion of something into a digital asset.

To understand tokenization, let's consider the example of a coffee beans business. The coffee beans you sell are of a very high quality and the value of the coffee increases by 10% each year. To tokenize your coffee business, you can assign value to a certain quantity of beans. Let's say you print 10,000 tokens and decide that one token is equal to 100 gram of coffee beans.

Now, let's say you want to offer these tokens to investors. The popular way of doing this would be to implement a smart contract on the Ethereum blockchain. The algorithm that will be implemented here will define all the attributes of your token. Now, you are on a platform that supports smart contracts and can encourage people to buy and sell your tokens.

In terms of the name for the token, it will have the name that you choose for it (let's call the token CB) and the name that relates to the underlying blockchain. Since it's powered by Ethereum the tokens will be ERC 20 tokens, which are tokens designed and used on the Ethereum platform only.

Tokenization offers different benefits. The transactions with your tokens are part of an immutable public ledger, so you don't have to worry about anyone questioning your or anyone else's ownership of their tokens. Also, compared to traditional methods, tokenization is cost efficient, with negligible administrative costs related to transactions of the coins. Another thing that tokenization offers partial purchase – you can purchase a portion of the asset you are selling if you can't afford the whole thing.

Types of Tokens

Three common types of tokens are currency tokens, utility tokens, and security tokens.

Currency Tokens

Bitcoin is an example of a currency token. These tokens do not have an asset linked to them like the above example of coffee. Instead these tokens get their value from their distribution system. The main purpose of currency tokens is to enable users to trade tokens and buy stuff with tokens.

Security Tokens

Security tokens that are sold as an investment opportunity, with expectation of profit, and assurance that the authority behind the tokens well be able to keep the business profitable. these 3 conditions are those given in the hobby test Howey Test Used by the US security and Exchange Commission (SEC).

Utility Tokens

Utility tokens help a company develop the product connected to the token. In other words, by buying the token you will be helping the company developed the product. In return you will get access to the product. People buy utility tokens with the expectation that these tokens will become more valuable as the product increases in demand in the market.

Challenges with Tokenization

A challenge with tokenization is that it is supposed to be following the law, but in reality, this is difficult to do. Smart contracts do not have a legal status at present. Also, the investors should be protected by regulations in case the underlying asset, in our case coffee beans, gets destroyed or stolen. Understanding these circumstances, some companies choose to sell legally compliant security tokens through Security Token Offerings (STOs).

STOs maybe the answer to the problems faced by initial coin offerings (ICOs). ICOs were all the rage not so long ago, and companies were offering tokens linked to anything and everything. To justify their projects, many of these companies claimed to sell utility tokens instead of security tokens. In the US, the SEC cracked down on these projects and declared vast majority of them to be securities in the eye of the law. Of course, the problem with being a security was that these tokens would be regulated as a security now. STOs can be a solution to this problem because they are backed by real assets and comply with regulatory requirements. However, regulatory requirements specific to digital currencies don't exist in most parts of the world, so the status of STO's is still to be decided.

Difference b/w Cryptocurrencies, Altcoins and Tokens

While you may hear some people using these three terms interchangeably, in reality there are differences among the three.

A cryptocurrency is any currency used for making or receiving payments on the blockchain. It is the broadest of the three terms. In comparison, an altcoin is the term used for coins that were alternative to the main player in the cryptocurrency market when they started coming out – Bitcoin.

Altcoins were promoted as coins that improve upon the Bitcoin project. Bitcoin Cash and Litecoin are two examples of altcoins. In comparison to these two tokens, crypto tokens are tokens that have their own blockchain and are connected to an asset or utility.

CHAPTER 4
APPLICATIONS OF
THE BLOCKCHAIN

Blockchain has wide ranging applications, from digital identity management to automated governance. Let's look at some of the applications of blockchain technology.

Smart Contracts
The most obvious application is digital transactions with the help of smart contracts. Blockchain enthusiasts are approaching smart contracts in different ways. Some startups are looking to create side chains connected to a larger public blockchains for offering specific types of transactions. Others are working on using documents stored in blockchains to complement legal agreements.

Example: One of the projects looking to advance smart contracts is the Cardano public blockchain. The project has a declared goal of "developing a smart contract platform which seeks to deliver more advanced features than any protocol previously developed." Cardano uses a PoS system and is working towards becoming an "Internet of Blockchain." In other words, the platform will allow all cryptocurrencies to co-exist and you will be able to convert from one to another without intermediaries. You will also be able to include metadata, which will make the transactions friendlier to governments and banks.

Healthcare

The nature of smart contracts means that they can also find used in the healthcare sector. You could create health records of patients and store them in a way that only those who have the private key can access the information. The public record could also be used for managing health care supplies and analyzing test results.

Decentralizing healthcare will also help to reduce the time between patients needing and getting health care. With data being available on a public ledger, the referral process between different healthcare providers will become smoother and as a result patients can expect faster care delivery.

Some of the main players in the smart contracts in healthcare market include Factom, IBM, Patientory, SimplyVital Health, PokitDok, smart-

Data Enterprises, FarmaTrust, Microsoft Corporation, etc. The blockchain-based smart contracts is segmented into Bitcoin, Ethereum, NXT and Sidechains.

Example: An example of the use of blockchain tech in combination with AI can be seen at Intermountain Healthcare. Based in Utah, the medical group has 22 hospitals. Intermountain is using the technology combo to identify waste, finding better outcomes for patients, and reducing costs, according to a Forbes article by Andrea Tinianow.

To get these benefits, the medical group used the blockchain based solution of BurstIQ and AI offerings of Empiric Health. According to BurstIQ CEO, Frank Ricotta, the company solved two fundamental healthcare industry problems: ability to support data and secure the underlying data. BurstIQ's allows for "granular data ownership, data sovereignty, and privacy, as well as accessibility of data across a highly complex set of stakeholders: patients, health systems, insurers, government agencies, biopharma, digital health solution providers and medical researcher communities. And they do all of this securely and at scale," according to the article.

Identity Management
The identity encryption aspect of blockchain has various applications as well. It can be used to create digital passports. Another future application

for personal identification could be a block chain ID that replaces all your current IDs, keys, etc.

Example: One of the projects in this field was launched in GitHub by Chris Ellis in 2014. According to Ellis, the aim of the projects is "to learn and layout a simple process for anyone in the world to create their own Private Passport Service that can be used to validate and prove the existence of other persons using nothing but available tools," as reported in this TechCrunch article. You can read more about the project here.

An issue with current identity management systems is that the information is often bought and sold for marketing purposes. Having a universal blockchain identity will mean that you don't have to provide your personal information to anyone for registration, shopping or identification. The immutable nature of blockchain ledger means that there will be less need for repeatedly verifying people through a tedious process. The record of each person will be accurately recorded and stay consistent overtime.

Example: Another way blockchain is changing marketing by removing the ability to get customer data for digital marketing without offering the customers anything in return. One of the solutions that is doing this is the Brave browser. The browser gives users the option of viewing ads and get Basic Attention Tokens (BATs) in return.

When you join their rewards program, your browser automatically starts keeping score of the attention you give to sites. The private ads appear as notifications, usually in the right side of your screen, and are not embedded in the content you are watching. Brave shares 70% of the ad revenue with you. Since the ad matchmaking happens on your device and not on the site you're visiting, there is no need to collect your personal information.

Brave has recently been in the news because it has accused Google of using hidden web pages for providing personal data of its users to advertisers. The profiling of users done by Google resulted in targeted ads. The company submitted the info to the Irish regulatory authority, and it claims that this act of Google is against EU privacy regulations.

Government
At the governmental level, blockchain can have several applications, from transparent voting to identification of immigrants. Encrypted wallets can reduce the risk of someone hacking into the system and manipulating elections. Moving government-related processes like taxation and voting to the blockchain will streamlines these processes. In case of immigrants coming into the country, a blockchain-based identity could be issued to people who don't have other form of identification, so they can perform transactions

without the need for cash in hand. It's important to note that a large percentage of the world's population is without basic documentation we take for granted. The blockchain could help provide a form of identity to these people, so they can use services, like healthcare and banking, that required a form of identification.

Example: Speaking of digital ID programs by governments, Joel Greenberg, a Seminole County, Florida, Tax Collector has created a private company, Government Blockchain Systems LLC, on July 19, to migrate information to an encrypted data base with the help of blockchain technology, according to gt news. According to Greenberg, the government's office is looking to use blockchain tech in a pilot program for launching a digital ID program in 2020. Greenberg "hopes to market it and lease the blockchain-based system and virtual ID to other local governments across the country as a joint venture with other private companies," the article mentions.

Finance
Another area where the blockchain can have a telling influence is the finance market. It's interesting to see that the digital revolution hasn't had a big impact on the financial sector. Although banks offer the convenience of performing transactions online, they haven't still managed to streamline the process of cross-border banking. This is the reason why intermediaries like Western Union are still a big

player in the finance market when it comes to cross-border transactions.

Example: The ability to prevent doubles-spending and counterfeits is an important attribute of digital currencies when it comes to their use in banking and finance. The blockchain provides these benefits. Developers are working on financial instruments that incorporate the attributes of the blockchain. For example, the open-source DOA project, launched in 2016 on the Ethereum blockchain, emulated crowdfunding. With DOA, the amount a person spent had a direct impact on how much say they would have in how the collected money would be spent. The largest crowdfunding in history, the DOA crowdfunding took place in May 2016.

Unfortunately, the project could not continue for long. One month after the historic crowdfunding, hackers were able to steal one-third of the collected funds. Later that year, DAO was delisted from Kraken and Poloniex exchanges.

Example: The DOA example is one in which blockchain technology, or problems with the code, resulted in a negative outcome. There are many examples where blockchain technology is being used successfully in the finance sector. Coin desk recently reported Bank of America's joining of Marco Polo, a consortium built on the Corda blockchain platform of the startup R3, which is a founder of the consortium, along with the startup TradelX. Marco Polo aims to make international trade more efficient with the help of blockchain technology.

"We look forward to exploring how the new technology can generate greater transparency for our clients throughout the transaction lifecycle, making traditionally paper-based, opaque processes easier and more efficient," stated Geoff Brady, who heads global trade and supply chain finance. Mastercard has also recently joined the consortium.

Example: Financial industry giant JP Morgan has launched its own cryptocurrency project. In Feb this year, the bank announced that they are "the first U.S. bank to create and successfully test a digital coin representing a fiat currency." The value of the JPM coin is equal to $1. Being on the blockchain, the coins can be sent instantaneously as it reduces the settlement time of transactions.

The type of coin offered by JP Morgan is called a stable coin. Stable coins are backed by fiat-based currencies. As mentioned above, the collateral in the case of JP Morgan coin is 1:1 in fiat currency. This ratio is different for different stable coins. The JPM coin is powered by the Quorum blockchain, which is JP Morgan's version of the Ethereum blockchain. The bank announced a partnership with Microsoft Azure to update Quorum.

Deutsche Bank is a recent signatory of the JP Morgan's blockchain project in an effort to lower costs. The Interbank Information Network (IIN) is led by JP Morgan and has 320 members who agree on sharing information on global payments through the blockchain.

Internet of Things (IoT)

Blockchain technologies are not only suitable for humans but also for things we use in our everyday life. The technology can be used to track the enormous number of connected devices and facilitate communication between these devices. In practical terms, it would mean that a person with a blockchain based identity could connect with an object (a door, car, etc.) having a digital identity without the need for a third party.

BITCOIN

Introduction

October 31st last year was the 10th year anniversary of the bitcoin's white paper release by Satoshi Nakamoto, who could be a single person or a group, no one knows. The white paper mentions "the need for an electronic payment system based on cryptographic proof instead of trust." This system would allow anyone "to transact directly with each other," thus eliminating third party involvement.

While we don't know much about Nakamoto, we do know about the works he used for developing the concept. In the references section, you can find a work of Stuart Haber and Scott Stornetta on digital timestamps and a work of Haber, Stornetta, and Dave Bayer on the same subject. Satoshi used the data structure from the former study to ensure that the timestamp server takes the hash of a block and timestamps it before broadcast. The importance of having the timestamp is that it proves existence of data before the hash.

Another book referenced in the Bitcoin wallpaper is

that of well-known cryptographer Dr. Adam Back. Dr. Back Has the distinction of inventing the hashcash, a proof of work algorithm that has become synonymous with Bitcoin. the hashcash algorithm is used as a denial of service counter measure. The algorithm requires completion of work and the proof of completion of work is verifiable. In terms of denial of service attacks, the attacker would need to do a lot of computational work if they want to affect how the recipient receives the message.

As mentioned earlier in the book, Bitcoin uses the concept of Merkle trees to verify data. The concept is named after its inventor Dr. Ralph Merkle. In a Merkle tree, the Merkle root provides a single hash which is used to verify transactions. The Merkle root is a combination of all the hashes of transactions related to the block. This structure allows verification of all transactions individually.

The History of Bitcoin

Bitcoins trading history is a history of optimism, controversy, recovery. The fight for acceptance the currency at the government level is still on, as the currency against acceptance among investors and businesses in various sectors slowly warm up to cryptocurrencies. Of course, the history of the blockchain was tied to the history of Bitcoin for the first few years when the crypto currency was introduced. While the blockchain has found used with other types of currencies, Bitcoin has remained the market leader in terms of total investment. Let's look at important landmarks in the history of the crypto currency.

Trading History of Bitcoin

The Start of Bitcoin

Collectively called the "genesis block," the first 50 bitcoins were born on Jan 9, 2009. To test the block-chain, the first bitcoin transaction was carried out a few days later, when Satoshi Nakamoto sent 10 BTC to a computer scientist called Hal Finney. The same year Bitcoin software became publicly available and people started mining the coin.

Bitcoin gets Value

In 2010, the first sale of Bitcoin took place, with the seller Laszlo Hanyecz, a virtual currency devel-oper, paying 10,000 BTC for two pizzas. To remem-ber this milestone, May 22 (day of the sale) is called Bitcoin Pizza Day. On Dec 12, Nakamoto separated from the project.

Altcoins Hit the Market

The release of Bitcoin led the way for other cryptos. By 2011, we saw other cryptocurrencies emerging. The new projects, also known as Altcoins, included Litecoin, whose initial release took place in Oct 2011.

Bitcoin Loses its Value

Shortly after reaching $1000 for the first time,

the price of Bitcoin started declining. In 2013, it dropped to around $300, and it took the currency another two years before reaching it rose to $1000 again.

2013 was a very Eventful year for Bitcoin. it also saw the temporary splitting of the blockchain into two parts, each with it's rules. but this was resolved after the developers halted transactions and most of the network return to the 0.7 version of Bitcoin. In Dec that year, China prohibited the use of bitcoins by financial institutions. This caused a drop in the cryptocurrency's value.

Bitcoins Scams

In 2014, Bitcoin became a lucrative means for criminals. In January 2014, Mt. Gox (the largest Bitcoin exchange in the world) suspended withdrawals and filed for bankruptcy. A reported $477 million in Bitcoins were stolen from the exchange. Former chief of the exchange, Mark Karpeles, pleaded not guilty to charges of embezzlement of funds. Note: Same year, Microsoft started accepting bitcoin for their Windows software and Xbox games.

Breaking Records

In 2015, Bitcoin reached an important landmark as the number of merchants accepting it crossed the 100,000 mark. Also, the same year Coinbase raised $75 mil in a Series C round, breaking previous records.

It was also the year when Bitstamp went offline to

investigate a hack which resulted in $5 mil worth of Bitcoins being stolen from their hot wallet. The exchange reopened after improving security and assuring customers that they would not be affected.

Bitcoin Reaches All-Time High Value

As places where Bitcoin could be spent continued to grow, its price continued to rise. The interesting part is that the price of Bitcoin in January 2017 was less than $3000, but by the end of 2019, the value of Bitcoin reached $20,000. Besides Bitcoin, the market cap of other crypto coins also increased. The total volume of the increased from $11bn to over $300bn.

A Rough Year for Bitcoin

In 2018, the price of Bitcoin dropped below $3,732, a big loss for Bitcoin users

Bitcoin Foundation

The Bitcoin foundation is a non-profit corporation modeled on the Linux foundation. Supported by companies that use Bitcoin technology, the foundation was created in Sep 2012 with the goal of restoring Bitcoin's reputation and promoting and protecting the cryptocurrency's decentralized, distributed, and private nature. Besides 84 lifetime members, the foundation also had 317 members who chose to stay anonymous, and many corporate members, including CoinLab, Gyft, and Mt. Gox. In its initial years, Bitcoin became the choice of different organizations; however, because of the way it works, the blockchain also allegedly became a choice of criminals who used it for laundering money.

The foundation hired Gavin Anderson, former lead developer of Bitcoin, on the position of chief scientist. Between 2012 and 2014, the foundation incurred significant losses. According to their IRS-990 forms, most of the funds were used to pay Gavin Andresen's salary, which increased from $15k in 2012 to over $147k in 2014. The total payments of the foundation rose from $29k in 2012 to $1.1 mil in 2014.

Despite the formation of the foundation was based on reviving bitcoin's reputation, the foundation itself face challenges from outside and from within. In Jan 2014, Charlie Shrem, VC of the foundation, got arrested with the charge of aiding and abetting unlicensed money transmission by helping an online market by the name of Silk Road. He resigned from his position and pleaded guilty do they charge. Mt. Gox CEO Karpeles was a board member of the foundation. He resigned from the position after the Mt. Gox scandal of Feb 2014 mentioned above. In May 2014, the two vacant positions were filled by Brock Pierce, a venture capitalist, and Bobby Lee, CEO of BTC China.

The Feb 2015 elections was the beginning of the end for the foundation. The newly appointed board members got voted out. This, combined with other members nearing the end of their mandates, saw the foundation violating its by-laws and deciding that there won't be any other board elections. This unsettlement combined with a loss of reputation rendered the foundation useless. In Jul 2015, foundation board member and Freedom Investment Group founder Olivier Janssens announced the insolvency of the foundation in the near future. The Bitcoin Foundation still exists, but it does not have any influence on Bitcoin's present or future.

CHAPTER 6
HOW BITCOIN TRANSACTIONS WORK

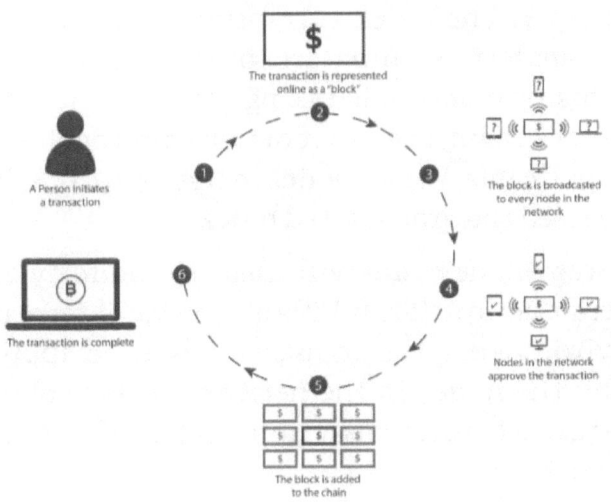

A Person initiates a transaction

The transaction is represented online as a "block"

The block is broadcasted to every node in the network

The transaction is complete

Nodes in the network approve the transaction

The block is added to the chain

STEP 1: PERSON A SENDS BITCOIN TO PERSON B.

Step 2: The transaction is propagated on the blockchain as part of a block.

Step 3: The block is transmitted to the nodes (transaction validators) of the network. Since this transaction is taking place on the Bitcoin blockchain, the proof of work protocol will be applicable and all nodes in the network will received the broadcasted block.

Step 4: The nodes will check the validity of the transaction. If it fulfills all the valid retreat environments, the transaction will be approved by the nodes in the network. This is also the stage where a transaction is rejected by the network.

Step 5: The validated and approved block is added to a chain of blocks. This block has an identifiable hash value. All the transactions within the block also have their own identifiable hash values. This way it is possible to Track the transaction. Each block is connected to the previous block as its hash value contains the hash value of the previous block as well. This is how the chains of the blockchain are formed.

Step 6: Person B receives the money sent by person A.

CHAPTER 7
BITCOIN FORKS

In the world of cryptocurrencies, Forks have become a common occurrence, this usually happens when adding new features to an established blockchain or to provide special security against hackers and cyberattacks, but it can also happen when developers have a different vision for the main project and take a different route, which often results in what is called a hard fork, in other words, a permanent split of the blockchain. This last scenario implies a change in the set of rules, thus creating a separate blockchain network. Bitcoin Forks are prime of example of this and they stem from changes in the source code of Bitcoin, resulting in incompatibilities that lead to the creation of a new type of Bitcoin.

Bitcoin Cash
The first hard fork of Bitcoin happened in on 1st of Aug 2017. It resulted from an attempt by

the bitcoin community to increase the number of transactions per second that the currency could handle. This meant increasing the size of the block from 1MB to 8MB. Many investors, developers, and miners pushed for this change, while many other members and bitcoin activists preferred to keep Bitcoin set of rules intact.

Eventually, this led to the creation of Bitcoin Cash (BCH). As a matter of reference, Bitcoin can handle 7 transactions per second, whilst Bitcoin Cash can average 61 operations per second. Nonetheless, these numbers are still far from competing with more traditional payment services, which are in the 1,000s of operations per second.

Differences b/w Bitcoin and Bitcoin Cash

Bitcoin Cash is the result of a long disagreement about the scalability of Bitcoin. The Bitcoin community believes in the use of SegWit, a method to separate the signature information from the transaction block. Meanwhile, the Bitcoin Cash community considers bigger transactions blocks will solve the issue of scalability. As a matter of fact, by May 2018, the block limit of the fork was increased to 32MB.

There are still some other significant differences that might go unnoticed by most people. For instance, the cryptocurrency employs a different transaction signature than Bitcoin. BCH has kept the P2P electronic cash as a feature, eliminating high fees and unreliable transactions. This is perhaps the greatest advantage that BCH has to offer to its end users, along with its significant speed increase over Bitcoin, making it possible to confirm transactions instantly.

Curiously enough, Bitcoin Cash has had its fair share of forks since its introduction, like Bitcoin Clashich, Bitcoin Candy and most notably, Bitcoin SV. When it comes to its market capitalization, Bitcoin Cash has remained as one of the most notable players, usually ranking in the top ten on the market cap list. The current the current market cap of the crypto currency is over $4.10 B, making it the fifth most popular crypto in the market.

Litecoin
During the cryptocurrency boom, another variant of Bitcoin began to gain strength. On paper, Litecoin is almost identical to Bitcoin Core. The cryptocurrency was created by Charlie Lee, an ex-Coinbase Engineering Director, and it was first published on GitHub on October 7, 2011, as an open-source project under the MIT/X11 license.

Difference b/w Litecoin and Bitcoin Cash
Litecoin is much easier to mine than Bitcoin, requiring less powerful equipment thanks to the implementation of Scrypt hashing algorithm in the PoW algorithm instead of SHA-256. Due to its ease of extraction, production is much higher than

that of Bitcoin. The processing time for Bitcoin is around 10 minutes, while the processing time for Litecoin is only two and a half minutes.

Scrypt is one of the most important features that differentiate Litecoin from Bitcoin. The Scrypt algorithm makes mining more expensive because it costs more to produce the Litecoin mining device compared to Bitcoin. The memory requirement is also higher due to the algorithm.

The price of Litecoin has never been as high as that of Bitcoin, but it has also never experienced the volatility associated with Bitcoin. Litecoin is in fact a very stable currency compared to some others with greater market caps. Its maximum price was $360 during the cryptocurrency boom in 2017. The current market cap of LTC is around $3.64 B and price over $57.

Bitcoin has also used Litecoin (LTC) to perform different tests with the Atomic Swaps system (a tool with which cryptocurrencies can be transformed).

Other Bitcoin Forks
There have been several other Bitcoin Forks as well, including Bitcoin XT, Bitcoin Classic and Bitcoin Gold. The XT emerged from the Bitcoin Core, and its purpose was to offer users an exponential increase in the size of the blocks, with a starting point of 8MB, and doubling in size every couple of years.

However, this was not well-received by the Bitcoin community. In 2017, XT became a Bitcoin Cash client by default with the release of its Release G version. Release G was updated twice with Release H and Release I to support the Bitcoin Cash protocol of 2017 and 2018 respectively.

Bitcoin Classic had the same origin but had a more abrupt end. In this case, it sought to solve a bottleneck that occurred with Bitcoin by constantly updating the consensus rules, and by increasing the size of the blocks to 2MB. The proposal started well with many companies and individuals supporting it, but after March 2016 the project began to decline to the point where in 2017 its operations ceased.

For its part, Bitcoin Gold is the one that has the most chance to succeed, especially since its change is based on the way the blocks are generated. Unlike Bitcoin, which uses the ASIC integrated circuit, the Bitcoin Gold uses the power of the GPU. In May 2018, about $18 million worth of Bitcoin Gold (BTG) was stolen from exchanges in a 51% hashing attack.

CHAPTER 8 TRADING BITCOINS

Options for Buying Bitcoin

Crypto exchanges function in a similar way to stock exchanges: they enable users to buy and sell bitcoin and other crypto assets. Two common types of crypto exchanges are crypto-to-crypto exchanges and fiat-to-crypto exchanges.

Types of Exchanges

Crypto-to-Crypto Exchange

These exchanges make it possible for customers to exchange cryptocurrencies such as Bitcoin (BTC), Ethereum (ETH), and Bitcoin Cash (BCH), etc. for other cryptos. Binance is an example of this type of exchanges.

Fiat-to-Crypto Exchange

With Fiat-to-crypto exchanges, customers can purchase cryptos and exchange them for fiat currencies. Coinbase is an example of this type of exchange.

Crypto Exchanges

Coinbase

Coinbase is one of the largest Bitcoin platforms. It serves as both a wallet and an exchange, making it a very easy place to begin with Bitcoin. Coinbase also supports Ethereum, Bitcoin Cash, and Litecoin. Funds can be transferred in and out of your account and then converted to Bitcoin. Coinbase charges 1% of the transaction, between $1 and $50. The Coinbase wallet is available through the mobile app or Web app or mobile app. The wallet is secured with a two-factor authentication and saves both digital and paper records of data. In a recent blog on their official website, Coinbase informed about the possible addition of 17 new cryptocurrencies to its current line up, including telegram and polkdaot.

Binance

Binance supports a wide range of digital currencies, including Bitcoin, Ethereum, and Binance's own coin BNB. For trades, Binance charges 0.1% as fees. The exchange makes it possible for users to trade coins into different currencies as well as offer support for digital currencies such as TRON, Litecoin,

Bitcoin Cash, EOS, Ethereum Classic, Ripple, Stellar Lumens, and many other lesser known cryptocurrencies.

Binance has very recently added to its fiat gateway channels. It's has partnered with payment processor Koinal to allow users to buy BTC, ETH, BCH, XRP and LTC with their Visa and MasterCard credit and debit card, and by wire bank transfer. According to Binance CEO, Changpeng Zhao, the goal of the partnership is to make crypto further into the mainstream. Before partnering with the London based Koinal, Binance partnered with Simplex, Trust-Token and Paxos For the same reason of including their channel into its fiat gateway.

Square Cash App

Square's Cash App is a mobile app where Bitcoin can be bought and sold with no fees. The app has already done well in assisting users to send money to their friends and family at no cost. Unlike some other digital wallets, your Bitcoin cannot be held outside of Square, rather it is held on your behalf in your Square Cash account for you to withdraw or sell.

If you trade stocks along with cryptos, then you may soon be able to do both with Square Cash. According to Bloomberg, Square is in the process of testing a new feature that would allow users to sell stocks for free.

Coinbase Pro

Coinbase Pro, initially referred to as GDAX, is an

easy-to-use trading platform, especially for those that are used to stock, option, and commodity trading platforms. Based on the trading volume of users, fees charged on this platform ranges from 0.10% to 0.30%.

Most people trade below $10 million each month and therefore will be included among the 0.30% tier. This platform is your best option if you wish to try Coinbase, but with a greater volume.

Robinhood

Robinhood began as a stock brokerage and has expand into the digital currency world. Robinhood, in Feb 2018, started supporting Bitcoin and Ethereum. The most attractive feature of the platform is that it requires no fees for selling and purchasing Bitcoin.

Robinhood stock is separate from Robinhood Crypto. Your account containing your stocks has your crypto coins as well. The app used to be just mobile-based, but now there's also a Web version of it in the market. At present Robinhood's use for crypto trading is limited to 16 states, so make sure you are in the right state before using it.

Tips for Trading

Bitcoin has a market cap of over $150B. While this may be small compared to the size of say the global equity markets, which is worth $23 trillion, it does constitute about 70% of the entire crypto market.

Bitcoin is the fundamental base of crypto markets and with blockchain-backed technology and distribution ledger, the coin is tradable 24/7 on multiple exchanges.

Volatility in the Bitcoin market provides numerous trade opportunities for long term and short-term traders. Here are some tips to trade Bitcoins.

Tip #1: Look out for the Fundamental News

Though most of the pro analysts would disagree with this statement, fundamental news does have an impact. Recall the Dec 2017 boom, it was highly related to the introduction of futures trading and anticipation of ETF approval. There are plenty of sites that provides relevant updates regarding Bitcoin on fundamental grounds, including Coindesk.com and Cointelegraph.com.

Tip #2: Volumes are Key

In any market, volumes play an important role in determining the next move of the underlying commodity. This applies to Bitcoin as well. With 200 exchanges and 24/7 operational markets, the chance of smart money coming into the pool can occur anytime. To deal with this, it is imperative you understand the daily volumes of top exchanges and for top coins too.

On-balance Volume (OBV) is one of the top technical indicators which you can use to detect smart money. The indicator uses an optimal mix of price and volume activity to determine when the smart money came into the flow. The uptrend of Bitcoin price and downward trend of OBV highlights the money has been pulled out from the market during the rally.

Tip#3: Understand Resistance and Support Levels

While history does not always repeat itself, still technical charts do tell a story and scrips mimic their old patterns. In order to understand the next move of any individual scrip, it is extremely crucial to understand the resistance and support levels of coins. CoinMarketCap carries the historic data for almost all cryptocurrencies and their trading view feature allows you to draw patterns on technical indicators. An understanding of resistance and support level would allow you to put stop loss in order to minimize their risks.

Tip#4: Diversification is Essential

The benefits of diversification hold true in cryptos as much as they hold true in case of traditional financial markets. Hence, a smart investor would always diversify their risks by investing a partial portion in Bitcoin and rest in alternative coins.

Tip#5: Stop Losses are Brakes you Can't Ignore

In a highly volatile market, stop-losses are the brakes that cover your risks and reduce the chances of maximum damage. Once you understand the resistance and support levels, playing with the trades is easy and becomes interesting as well. As we have discussed that coins do repeat a pattern, hence if you already know support of some coin, you would put a stop-loss above that range to keep your trade safe.

Secondly, stop-losses guard your profits. With a stop-loss, you can protect a significant chunk of profits while keeping only a minimal exposed to market risks.

Trading is not a study rather is an art which one can master only with consistent performance. Remember, there would be setbacks, days with no trades and some frustrations too, but a long-term trader always looks for new opportunities. And by following a pattern of rules, the risks of losing your capital can be reduced.

CHAPTER 9
GOVERNMENTAL
ACCEPTANCE

Crypto currencies have running run into problems with regulators because of how they work and the scams and scandals that the digital asset has experienced during its history. Regulating this new asset class is a challenge for regulatory bodies all over the globe, and governments are dealing with cryptocurrencies in different ways.

The US

To start let's look at the situation in the US. On Sep 19th, 2019, the House of Representatives passed a bill that calls for the financial crimes regulator FinCEN to study how the bureau can benefit from the use of blockchain and other technologies.

According to the bill, "The Director of the Financial Crimes Enforcement Network ("FinCEN") shall carry out a study on... whether AI, digital identity technologies, blockchain technologies, and other innovative technologies can be further leveraged to make FinCEN's data analysis more efficient and effective."

In a 24 Sep, 2019 hearing, the US House of Representatives Financial Services Committee, Financial Services chairperson Maxine Waters started by touching on a several SEC's activities and singling out Libra, stating "Facebook is looking to establish a new global financial system intending to rival the U.S. Dollar," according to this Coin Telegraph report.

Sure, this follows the ongoing questioning though All Facebook of Facebook off Facebook in relation to its controversial Libra cryptocurrency project. This questioning from within the USA Senate and has now spread normally who is global level they called off the lands of Facebook who monster currency at a global level. Facebook's privacy record is the main cause of concern in this project.

Regulators are thinking of Libra as security token which should be regulated as a security. Commenting on Libra, US regulators have said "The Libra Investment Token could amount to a security since it is intended to be sold to investors to fund startup costs and would provide them with dividends. The Libra token itself may also be a security, but Facebook does not intend to pay dividends and it is unclear if investors would have a "reasonable expectation of profits," according to a report by

Cryptovest.

Canada
According to the official website of Government of Canada, "You can use digital currencies to buy goods and services on the Internet and in stores that accept digital currencies. You may also buy and sell digital currency on open exchanges, called digital currency or cryptocurrency exchanges."

France
In France, cryptocurrencies are still largely unregulated, with two blockchain tech ordinances being the only legislative steps taken at present. However, in 2019, France announced new rules specifically for digital coins. The purpose of these rules is to enable firms dealing in cryptos to gain approval by following the consumer protection and finances-related standards voluntarily. This announcement follows a last year announcement in which Paris proposed rules for facilitating crypto-related businesses in the country.

According to information provided by the Library of Congress (LOC), in 2016, an ordinance with two provisions allowing blockchain tech use for mini-bonds came to the fore. This bond is a certain type of zero-coupon bond. The ordinance led to France defining "blockchain" in legal terms for the first time. This ordinance was followed by a 2017 for enabling the use of the technology in other financial instruments.

France plans to stop the use of Facebook's Libra in the EU. According to a report by The Independent, France's Economy and Finance Minister, Bruno Le Maire, says "I want to be absolutely clear: In these conditions, we cannot authorize the development of Libra on European soil."

"It would be a global currency, held by a single player, which has more than two billion users around the world. The monetary sovereignty of states is under states is under threat," he added.

China

According to the LOC, China is yet to pass a legislation for regulating cryptocurrencies. Regulators don't consider cryptocurrencies as "legal tender or a tool for retail payments." Banks do not provide any crypto-related services. ICOs are banned in the country. Crypto exchanges cannot convert legal tender into cryptocurrencies.

India

India does not have a regulatory framework for cryptocurrencies. Last year, the Indian government declared Bitcoin as not a legal tender in the country.

CHAPTER 10
FUTURE OF THE BLOCKCHAIN

This is a very interesting time for blockchain-based technologies. You can literally pick and industry and find ways in which blockchain can improve it.

Bitcoin and Ethereum

In terms of the application of blockchain technology, we can say that the cryptocurrency Bitcoin is still the leading solution we have seen. The cryptocurrency has a disproportionately large share in the market, and it looks like this is going to be the case in the near future as well. Because, logic says that for another crypto to go past Bitcoin, they must show that their brand, network, and features are better than what Bitcoin has to offer.

However, there are some serious contenders for the best application of blockchain tech if you look at the long term. One of these contenders is of course the Ethereum network. If you look at the difference in market cap in terms of Ethereum coins, the Ethereum blockchain has a market cap of 107,897,150 ETH while bitcoin is at 892,041,149 ETH. However, in terms of developers building on a particular blockchain, Ethereum is leading the pack. Just like bitcoin had the advantage of being first to market as a cryptocurrency. Ethereum has had the advantage of being first to market in terms of making it easy for developers to build decentralized applications.

It's fair to say that currently, Ethereum is going through and experimental phase that is incomparable to any other ecosystem, with projects in a variety of industries using their blockchain solutions. Some experts are saying that the result of this experimental phase will be good for Ethereum and it will achieve its scaling and privacy goals in the next few years. In comparison, bitcoin is starting to shift from the experimental phase to a building phase, where developers are focusing on building on the Bitcoin stack.

It's also important to note hear that while Bitcoin and Ethereum are market leaders, there are other players who are making strides. For example, the decentralized application platform Tron has more active users compared to Ethereum.

Mainstream Adoption
Of course, when we look at applications of the

blockchain, we must also consider projects started by the traditional industry. These projects have the potential to become leading applications of the blockchain technology fairly quickly because of the reputation and resources of their founders.

As mentioned earlier in the book, banking giant JP Morgan has developed its on blockchain-based solution. The reputation of the bank is a driving force behind other prominent financial institutions partnering with JP Morgan to take advantage of the benefits of their solution. Similarly, if social media giant Facebook manages to successfully launch its cryptocurrency Libra, it can become a global player and in fact change the game of money transfer itself. As with JP Morgan, we see that the position of Facebook in its industry can be used to garner support from major players. In the case of Libra, we see major corporations like Airbnb, MasterCard, Virgin Group, PayPal, and many other big names for different industries supporting the project.

Governmental acceptance will also be a crucial factor in how blockchain-based technologies prosper. Many governments are in the process of defining the blockchain and use of cryptocurrencies. At the same time, major world economies like China and India have placed a ban on the trade of cryptocurrencies. Considering the importance of cryptos when it comes to blockchain tech, encouragement from the government will play a defining role in the progress of blockchain technology in that country.

New Projects

Despite the challenges of scalability, security, and acceptance, the disruption is on its way. Here are some of the new projects promising to disrupt in their respective industries:

1. MetaMask

MetaMask is an add-on which allows you to access Ethereum based dapps in your browser without running a node. The browser has a native wallet which can be connected to multiple platforms and can be accessed accordingly. According to Meta-Mask, there were 1.1 million transactions in April 2019. Majority of transactions (63%) are taking place happening on the Ethereum Mainnet, but there's significant activity on Ethereum testnets as well. The company also recorded 71k transactions on networks that aren't Ethereum-based.

2. Augar

If you're a betting person who's looking for a peer to peer network for crypto wagers, then Augar is the platform for you. According to the official website: Augur is a set of smart contracts that can be deployed to the Ethereum blockchain. Any user who downloads and runs the Augur software has access to the Augur protocol on the Ethereum block-chain." In essence, Augar is an open source protocol that you can use to create your own prediction market.

The auger platform Allows you to back on a wide variety of markets, some crypto do sports. Creating your home prediction market is easy and just requires a few steps. Let's say you're betting on who will win the next election in your country. From your prediction market page for this question on Augar, you will be able sell And buy shares after off the outcome you predict of the election. if you're right in your prediction, you will get a payout in ETH sent to your Ethereum wallet.

3. Status

Status is a crypto wallet, messenger and Web3 browser with the goal of being a "secure communication tool that upholds human rights." With one of the most active team of developers on GitHub, Status is currently developing android, iOS and desktop versions of their app. The project is completely open source and has beta versions for their iOS and Android mobile apps and also for desktop for Windows, Mac and Linux.

4. Cosmos

Cosmos is a blockchain interoperability platform that is powered by the Tendermint consensus algorithm. According to there official website "Cosmos is an ecosystem of blockchains that can scale and interoperate with each other."

Cosmos aims to make it easy for developers to break barriers between blockchains. Their main objectives are to enable blockchains to maintain their sovereignty, perform transaction at a faster rate, and communicate with other blockchains. In their words, they want the project to result in an "Internet of Blockchains, a network of blockchains able to communicate with each other in a decentralized way."

CONCLUSION

The world was introduced to the concept of blockchain and cryptocurrency a little over a decade ago. In this relatively short period of time, we have seen a significant increase in the interest in these concepts, not only in developers and investors, but also the general public.

In this brief time period, we have seen the emergence of Bitcoin as an alternative to fiat currency. We have also seen the blockchain separating from Bitcoin and developing into competing blockchains. The success of Bitcoin has also led to the development of numerous other cryptocurrencies and tokens.

The blockchain and its applications have also started a debate among regulatory authorities about how to regulate the new asset class of cryptocurrencies. Judging from the interest of developers and investors in blockchain-based tech, we can safely say that this emerging technology is only going to spread in the coming days.

References

https://www.investopedia.com/tech/what-are-centralized-cryptocurrency-exchanges/

https://hackernoon.com/decentralization-versus-centralization-what-it-is-how-it-works-where-is-it-going-and-which-one-a725de8426ec

https://masternodes.com/chaincoin/

https://www.technologyreview.com/s/612974/once-hailed-as-unhackable-blockchains-are-now-getting-hacked/

https://www.techopedia.com/definition/1770/cryptography

https://www.lifewire.com/cryptographic-hash-function-2625832

https://www.ico.li/blockchain-validate-data/

https://www.binance.vision/blockchain/proof-of-stake-explained

https://blockgeeks.com/guides/different-smart-contract-platforms/

https://blockgeeks.com/guides/smart-contracts/

https://cointelegraph.com/explained/tokeniza-tion-explained

https://thenextweb.com/hardfork/2019/05/01/cryptocurrency-stolen-first-quarter-2019-hack/

https://www.finder.com/no/cryptocurrency/wal-lets

https://hackernoon.com/a-huge-list-of-cryptocur-rency-thefts-16d6bf246389

https://www.vox.com/re-code/2019/5/8/18537073/binance-hack-bitcoin-stolen-blockchain-security-safu

https://www.blockchaintechnologies.com/appli-cations/

https://thenextweb.com/hardfork/2019/09/04/brave-google-chrome-browser-track-users-hidden-web-pages-gdpr/

https://brave.com/brave-rewards/

https://cointelegraph.com/news/bitcoin-white-paper-10-years-since-satoshis-vision-was-brought-to-life

https://breakermag.com/money-was-the-sizzle-blockchain-pioneer-w-scott-stornetta-assesses-satoshis-work/

https://101blockchains.com/who-is-satoshi-nakamoto-bitcoin/

https://www.investopedia.com/articles/forex/041515/countries-where-bitcoin-legal-illegal.asp

https://techcrunch.com/2019/05/14/bitcoin-shrug-emoji/

https://www.bitwala.com/what-is-bitcoin-trading/

https://www.france24.com/en/20181023-rise-fall-suspense-bitcoins-wild-first-decade

trading.https://www.investopedia.com/tech/how-to-buy-bitcoin/

https://www.thebalance.com/best-places-to-buy-bitcoin-4170081

https://en.m.wikipedia.org/wiki/History_of_bitcoin

https://www.ig.com/en/bitcoin-btc/how-to-trade-bitcoin

https://blockgeeks.com/guides/how-to-trade-bitcoin/

https://en.wikipedia.org/wiki/Bitcoin_Foundation#cite_note-Guardian-1

https://cryptoslate.com/bitcoin-foundations-meteoric-rise-collapse/

https://www.coindesk.com/house-legislation-blockchain

https://in.reuters.com/article/us-crypto-curren-cies-regulation-france/france-to-approve-first-crypto-issuers-as-new-rules-loom-idINKC-N1UB18P?il=0

https://www.bbc.com/news/business-49008298

https://libra.org/en-US/white-paper/?noredirect-=en-US

https://www.loc.gov/law/help/cryptocurrency/world-survey.php

https://www.techradar.com/news/china-set-to-launch-its-own-cryptocurrency

https://www.vantageasia.com/imc-ban-crypto-currency-india/

https://www.coindesk.com/france-says-it-will-block-facebook-libra-in-europe-report